BEAUTIFUL GIRLS

Melissa Lee-Houghton was born in Wythenshawe, Manchester in 1982. Her poetry, short fiction and reviews have been published in literary magazines such as *Succour*, *The Short Review*, *Magma* and *Tears in the Fence*. Her first collection, *A Body Made of You*, was published in 2011. She lives in Blackburn, Lancashire.

ALSO BY MELISSA LEE-HOUGHTON

*A Body Made of You* (Penned in the Margins, 2011)

# Beautiful Girls

## Melissa Lee-Houghton

Penned in the Margins

LONDON

PUBLISHED BY PENNED IN THE MARGINS
Toynbee Studios, 28 Commercial Street, London E1 6AB
www.pennedinthemargins.co.uk

The right of Melissa Lee-Houghton to be identified as the author of this work has been asserted by her in accordance with Section 77 of the Copyright, Designs and Patent Act 1988.

First published 2013

ISBN
978-1-908058-03-4

# CONTENTS

## ACKNOWLEDGEMENTS

I would like to thank the following magazines in which versions of these poems have previously appeared: *3:AM*, *Under the Radar*, *Hearing Voices*, *Poems In Which*, *The Prague Revue*, *The White Review*, *Fit To Work*, *The Quietus*, *The Screech Owl*, *Ink, Sweat & Tears*, *Astronaut* and *Tears in the Fence*. The poem 'Home Leave' was Highly Commended in the Lupus UK Competition 2013. 'Town Show '82,' 'I'll Find You' and 'Bringing You Home' were part of a collection that won The New Writer Collection Competition 2013. 'Bringing You Home' was published in *Sculpted: Poetry of the North West* (North West Poets, 2013).

I would also like to thank the following people for their help, support and encouragement: Rebecca Critchley, Jos Foster, Alexandra Gallagher, Lucy Gallagher, Karen Cooper, Betty Houghton, Doll Houghton, Neil Houghton, Sheila Hamilton, Bobby Parker, Eli Regan, Abegail Morley, Chris McCabe, Pascale Petit, David Caddy and Tom Chivers.

# Beautiful Girls

*Dedicated to my beautiful girls:*
*Elizabeth, Rebecca, Jade, Alexandra, Elysia & Evangeline*

# Heaven

Heaven is the place between the sky and the planets.
You have to soar through the clouds to reach it.
You go there if you have a personality disorder
or learning disability, or if you made all three appointments
in a row. The drugs give you extra lift
as you go. When you get there
you can be invisible. You spend most of your life
that way — it's a comfort. Only now you never cry
and you don't need anyone to watch you cling to life.
Heaven is the place where we spend eternity, amazed
that life has to happen at all;
the place where we are unnoticed and learn to sing songs
backwards and spell out names in languages
no-one uses. We don't have to worry about our insides
or being mistaken for someone else. Being forgotten
is beautiful. Being forgotten has not always been beautiful.

# Beautiful Girls

In our graves we are all
beautiful girls. Our skin
is falling away like the tide.
Our bones are
long and slender,
all inhibitions gone. We're
lovely in the mud
that fit boys have dug
for a council wage,
not knowing how beautiful
we lay there
like honeymoon brides
anticipating sex,
not expecting death —
serene as pawns and queens
and home in ourselves
forever.

# Sixteen

The red velvet coat meant I was not for sale, but bought.
Its fur trim was part of the illusion, and one month in
to my living away from home it garnered a stain
which no washing machine would ever clean. Just say
you were a doll and someone owned you and petted you
and you wanted to wake up but your eyes never closed.
Just say you were wearing red because you loved the sunset;
not because it clung to your body like a bin bag on a wet corpse
and your femininity was misinterpreted. Just say death
was in and out of your mouth. I wore black boots
that didn't need lacing, and I wasn't going anywhere.
They were no good for winter, no good for snow, no good
for running home. I remember I used to count up the loose change
for cigarette papers. I would go out in my red velvet
to the chip shop and barter for a bag of salted fat.
I was good for roasting. I was good for roasting.
My face was like a slot-machine. I make sure
we never drive through that town now, in case I see her —
a girl in a red velvet coat and boots that don't lace, thumbing
a ride. I wouldn't take her anywhere.
I wouldn't know *where* to take her.

# Hunger Pangs

Skinny girls try to cut into their arms with blunt knives.
Sunita is eating out of the food disposal.
They take flight, run to the bathroom, scrambling
past each other to be the first.
I look at my plate and feel guilty for my hunger pangs.
Sunita has clods of food in her soft, dumpy hands.
They drag her on her behind, down the corridor,
her big mammal laugh booming. This madness in me,
it is of a timbre that leaves my emotions emaciated.

*I cannot cry; these girls are beautiful and dying.*
*I cannot cry; nobody is going to save me. Not here.*

The sunsets are like nothing else, they move me to tears,
though I watch from my reinforced window. No-one cares
about the fucking sun.
When it's dark, no-one's sorry.
Trees lash the windows like we're in *Wuthering Heights*
and the gale force winds don't mean nothing at all.
They're no match for thirteen girls
who can handle the sight of blood
and will fly out into the night.

# Asylum Girls

The girls would run and hide, would run around
trying to catch chickens, beside themselves with laughter.
The girls would throw eggs in the yard, write graffiti and curse.
In the dormitory, the girls would squeal when a male nurse

came in. They secretly wished
he'd stay and watch them sleep.
The girls would snore and snort ever so quietly.
The girls would hatch plans, would write letters in code.

The girls would torment the boys, and run to the toilet after meals.
The girls would covet glass and razorblades. The girls would wear
one another's clothes; they would shave each other's heads.
The girls would stop at nothing.

The girls swallowed glass. They ran off hand in hand.
The girls were found by the police.
The girls were taken to the infirmary in riot vans.
The girls would count out paracetamol. They would share if necessary.
The girls listened to rock songs and danced around in socks and skirts.

The girls had been abused, the girls had been misunderstood.
The girls had been put there under false pretences. The doctors
fell in love with the girls. The nurses fell in love with the girls.
Madness was attracted to the girls, as they were to madness.

The girls were damaged.
The girls were not in love.
The girls were vicious.
The girls were exceptional.
The girls wished they were not girls.

# Jade

They called me at three o'clock in the afternoon to tell me
you'd no longer be able to call me at three o'clock in the morning
to ask me what day it is, that you'd no longer be able to go out with me
to a bar like a fishbowl with bull sharks circling;
that you'd never again make love to me in the woods
or drop acid and sit in the sunshine writing songs and talking to God.
I didn't call you the night that you passed; the police broke down the door
and there you were. Honey, you shaved off all your hair.

I followed you,
one hundred yards ahead and walking heavy, slow. I went into a trance;
you took me all the way to the cemetery where your grave was still crowned
with a thousand lovely petals, not the barbed wire you'd have asked for.
I felt a halo of surging sunlight glow. I could feel your bones beneath me.
I could feel that you were gone, that you didn't want to come home.

I remember your perfect cheekbones; your pliable, wonderful skin;
how you would squeeze me tight and bury me in.
Now when I go to the cemetery an Arctic wind blows up my dress,
your mum never neglects your grave. Yes baby
we all had lessons to learn. No more would you rouse
from your sleep, imploring me, *what did I miss, what did I miss?*

# Anarchy

The cold grips our skin. We run
around the football pitch
at ten pm in the middle of winter.
The dark is playful with us,
giving us shape and silhouette.
Some guy parks his car on the driveway
and we shout over;
he hurries inside his house and we figure
we'd better put some clothes on.
We could be made of ice. We don't care.
As far as we're concerned, if aliens land
*this* is where they will land —
and in our glory, we dance.

Jade lives above an old launderette.
The gorgeous steam smell of the place gets
up our sensitive noses and in our hair.
Her mum plays Rush LPs, wears
leather skirts and takes Prozac.
In the evening we can't go into the living room
in case she's skinning up.
One time her dad came into the room,
and talked to her guitar like it was a person.
We laugh, though I know her life is tragic.
I walk by her in school and my nipples hurt;
I want to touch her all the time.

We try on sunglasses in a department store
on a day out by the sea.
We run out of the shop wearing them
streaming with tears of laughter.
It gives us a hunger; we buy greasy doughnuts
and walk the promenade, hand in hand.
Nobody stares.
We can do no wrong. We can get stoned
in the woods and make out, and no-one
stops us. We can sleep together like release doves.
At times we feel insane,

so we drink our tinnies and smoke cigarettes,
talk about leaving school and working in telesales.
Talk about the flat we'll have together
and the pets, and the music we will listen to all night.
(We won't need to sleep;
we're of the darkness, our eyes need never shut.)
Her mum falls asleep in the chair
in her dressing gown, or comes in pissed
and tripping and she carries her to bed.
We have found ways of hiding from this.
Vodka does the trick, and sex.
But it's not the way they do it in the movies.

We have hard hearts.
We share t-shirts, jeans, spit.
All the lads fancy her but she never even blinks.
I have her, only I can turn her head

and I'm mad with it.
We drink wine through straws by the woods.
We are on a higher plane.
Her eyes are blue like a husky's.
Her pupils are always tiny.
Her skin is so supple and firm;
she is a wild creature, and I won't tame her.
Her heart beats double time when I'm sleeping.
I don't know what I'm doing with her.

She writes me letters, I read them in bed.
She says she's crying, says she's lonely.
Says she's had to put her mum to bed again.
Says she's not going to school anymore,
they'll have to make her, and all I see
are the highlighted words in the final paragraph:
*please baby always love me.*

# In My Sleep I Try To Wake You

We drive to the outskirts
where the fog is blistering the sky.
You have to take the wheel
when its axle throws out of control
because my heart is thumping;
I can see colours at the back of my eyes
the world is the colour of pig's liver —
there's a sheen over everything
as though something violent just happened,

and then I think I taste blood.
You don't want me to crash but you don't want to
look at me either.
You say you're ashamed,
that there's no appeasing a bad conscience,
a fractured mind,
and yours folded with the addiction.

We drive to your parents' through the morning.
There's a big bottle blue pool and we dive in
but parts of you begin to turn black
and nobody knows who I am.
I try to make them see that you're back but they
throw me my clothes and send me on my way;
they act like you're not there.

I don't see you for days.
I call your mobile every five minutes,
the urgency making me vomit.
When at last you call back you are
lying in an open glass coffin, waiting.
I laugh at you
you don't budge and you're cold but you see me,
I know you do.
You have closed your eyes to me and pulled out all your nails.
I slap you around the face again, and again, and again.

# Sundown by the Abattoir

We are falling down; it's summer; we are falling through time
worn thin. Summer is wasted, is pale and screwed up
in the clouds above our childhood town
and our dizzy heads.

      Nobody trusts a blue sky.
I am too good to be true and you are too good to be true.
(Last night I dreamt I fell in love all over again
and when he kissed me I woke with a start.)

I feel there is nothing more intact than your mind.
Mine is lost. Things up there are loose.
I walked down by the abattoir with the kids —
I said, *kids, this is where they kill the cows and lambs*

*and chop them into mince-meat.*
One didn't believe me and the other didn't care.
The sun was sagging in the sky.
We held hands to cross the roads.

They've dismantled the phone box by the abattoir;
the one I used to ring you on with 20p coins,
when sometimes you just hung on the line and I'd
hear you breathing and grip the receiver.

Do you know how exquisite that sadness was?

You would lie in bed, half-asleep, drowning in it.
I don't know why I needed you, I never knew.
After you vanished, I worked at the abattoir one winter

when I couldn't afford bedclothes or hot food.
The girls there nearly skinned me alive. I got free
and the smell and colour of raw meat still drains me.
The sun's going down now darling. There's a rare pink sky;

I have just read your email
about the Indian boy you got drunk,
about buying Scandinavian furniture
and how you'd like to be there for me.

I have your number programmed into my phone
just in case anything bad happens. The sun is going down slow,
the sky looks beaten. I need you to know,
simply your being alive consoles me.

# Virginity

Underneath their books on *Star Trek*, and *A Brief History of Time*,
catalogues open on the underwear pages,
men's groins in tight underpants.
Two boys. Not footballers, not carpenters, or soldiers or electricians.
Not like the other boys.
They'd sit in each other's rooms drinking Vimto
and programming computers, the only two
who had them. They had the internet and they spent
all their time devoted to it. We would go round to their houses
and they would boast, *Type in anything you want,*
as though they were the genies of these virtual lamps.

We got drunk on Malibu and gin at Paul's mother's
while she was out for the day one summer.
Paul drank loads, said his brother abused him and it made him gay.
He showed us pornography that his friend in London sent —
and I couldn't take my eyes off it.
I walked six miles home in the baking sun, pissed,
developed sunstroke. While I shivered and burned on the sofa
they came to see if I was ok
and I cried until they had to leave.

I had these feelings that I wanted someone to fuck me.
I wanted to be fucked and I wanted it to be quick
and then I wanted to lie in a hot bath and wash it all away,
this fledgling desire suffering inside my body without love.

# Codeine

You haven't written in six months, O terror of terrors, O clot of dark in my heart.
I write to you still, and it reaches you somehow, like the smattering of rain
that hits the bus window as you stare out over the landscape. That's me.
And the football those kids booted in your belly. That was me too.
You don't get to escape from me, I have a lifetime of haunting to do.
I saw a picture of you; your hair hasn't fallen out, you still squint through glasses.
Your headaches turn into my headaches. When the paracetamol doesn't take the
edge off, that's you. When I'm reaching for the codeine, that's you.
And I would punch you in the head if you were here, in the flesh.
It's called progress. I am not waiting for a letter. You are not waiting for a letter.
It comforts me to think you read my books. You read them and you suffer
little paper-cuts. You read them and your temples bruise. I wish you no harm.
Sometimes I wish you would write, but I'm afraid there's nothing so delicate
as that, O moonbeam, O poet in the night, O honest miracle. Now I exist
leagues from your heart. I still find your poems hidden between the pages of my
books, toying with the idea of making my love-hearts leap. I read them in my own
voice, not yours. Yours is caught somewhere between the tide and the mountains
of rain-cloud. O my mute harbinger, O danger, you will never remember
thirst, or the taste of me and the gutted sea.

# Tough Guys

We contracted influenza when I was seven or eight and slept,
my older sister, my mother and I,
in the maternal bed under one set of plain white sheets,
wet through with sweat, our feet touching.
As we got better, grandma turned the television on
and we saw an advert for oven chips, which she procured
and we ate in bed, smothered in ketchup, licking and licking
the salt off our fingers.

My mother would answer the door on a Saturday morning
in a t-shirt. No underwear, no bra.
The kid would ask if I was playing out and she'd invite them in,
her shiny shaved legs embarrassing me.
She'd smoke at the sink, and I'd abhor the smell,
those years when separation
came hand in hand with smoking cessation:
hidden packets of cigarettes and patches, paraphernalia.
She did it in the end,

and she learned how to wear mascara and heels
and pyjamas, and dyed her hair, and we couldn't
keep up with all the changes in her.
One day she was chopping carrots and cut her finger.
We were ushered out of the room but I wanted to see
blood the blood the blood the blood,
just to know she was fallible, and that we didn't have to believe

she'd live forever. I needed to know we could let go,
that it was possible to be apart from her
without my chocolate eardrums
and my sand-pit heart and my play-dough tongue

bursting.

# No-one Touches Me

I go to the Underground just so that someone with a heart
rubs up against me. My heart is an eye and it sees heat
in colour. I'm filled with pink noise, and in the drone of trains
and voices I want to slip my hand into someone else's pocket.
Tonight, I won't dream, because nobody
has held me and no hands have strayed and even
though I'm drunk with love, my arms are empty.

When I was little I used to draw
pictures of men and women kissing.
An older girl taught me how to French kiss —
it was very wet but I wanted to do it all day.
We slept together happily in a caravan parked
in my nana's driveway. These days when I see her in the street
with her husband she avoids me.

When they told me I was mad, nobody wanted to touch me
in case it infected them too. The doctor had my mother
and father put their arms around me so I couldn't move
and I squealed and they shouted, is this necessary?
They didn't want to hold me and I didn't want to be held.
The doctor nodded his head solemnly as though he understood.
Later I gripped my pillow and prayed.

I think it was something people just got used to, the not-touching.
I tried going to Sunday Service, and nobody shook my hand —

I tried the swimming pool, but you're not supposed to
touch anyone on purpose there, they think you're a perv.
I tried dates in bars but they all swerved when I leaned in for a kiss.
You see, when I touch someone, I'm there —

right there in their body, like a disease or a shrill noise.
I put my hands on your body and you freeze.
I have you in me like cigarette smoke.
I place my hand on your chest and keep it steady.
This is too much for amateurs.
I need someone who can take it,
the guy whose armpit I'm currently beneath

on the Northern Line. I'm invading his space.
I could squeeze the life out of him
as soon as look at him.
Tonight, with limp arms I gather up the bedclothes
and sleep with them in a big heap, full and warm.
I don't undress for anyone. Nobody whispers my name
in my ear. I lie there with my body-of-bedding

and think of all the doctors whose hands I've shook
and whose pills I've swallowed and whose touch
I've craved and whose prescriptions I've obtained.
And I think of all the men running away
like gingerbread that I would beg to kiss me until I faint.

# Unfastened

She wore the conch-coloured blouse to restaurants and parties,
her maternal breasts filling and re-filling it with uneven breaths.
Even though you were only ten you knew the difference
between polyester and pure silk.
You'd rescue it from the linen basket, smother your mouth
and nose, the delirious smell of her skin, so often without
even a hint of sweat; she smelled the colour of honeysuckle.
Ashamed, after you'd tried it on for the mirror,
done the buttons up all wrong in the moment,
you stuffed it under your mattress where your hand
would reach down in the night to finger
those mother-of-pearl buttons so fiddly to undo,
your fleecy hair, like hers, falling over your face in your imagination.
When he found out, he said it was natural, which meant they'd notice
next time. Next time you would be with Sylvester Stallone
in the Garden of Eden, he'd have his arm around you, the silk
just rippling under his coin-sized fingertips.

# Blowjob

After a trip to the corner shop
for some cigarettes and a bag of razors
the girls move on to the red light district
where the jagged night excites them
and punters crawl up like crocodiles
eyeing up flesh, ready to roll.
They get in a car, a little blue run-around.
They say £20, but Debbie can't get it up
and Marie is still a virgin.
In the end, between them it's done and they share
a celebratory bag of salted chips
on a park bench at midnight in June.
Fella said they'd better get some practice
if they were gonna take it serious, like —
and from where they are sat they can see
the whole world, the whole night,
the whole sky rippling out from behind their heads:
stars, dynamite light, dripping with explosions.
Marie thinks for a moment
about alien life, and Debbie thinks for a moment
about love. All they have left
is a police ride back to the asylum
where they can take their scars
and their mental illnesses
and go fuck themselves

# Bodies

I left the body under the floorboards

in the bedroom.
I wanted it gone
but there was nowhere else
and every time I tried to lift it
flesh broke off in chunks.

I return to the body often
and stand there trying to find
a moment of inspiration.

I painted the room when I was nineteen.
I painted the floorboards
because I couldn't afford a carpet.

I hung mirrors and pictures
and it was so pretty

but now I wonder when
someone will notice the stink.
I didn't kill it you see,
I just found it.
I even kissed it
when I laid it there.

Now I peek under the floorboards every day
just to make sure it hasn't started breathing.
I wear white boots
and I'm ready to stamp on its face.

You tell me at the train station
in a quiet spot on the platform
that you have a body too,
hidden in your caravan,
and that you can't stop looking at it.

You're not sure how it even happened.

We sit together in silence
very cold; it's winter, harsh.
We yawn sometimes;
we are hyperaware
and yet preoccupied.
You talk about what you'll make for tea
and say you didn't eat yesterday.
I say it's no wonder we're off our food.
We laugh.
My body's tied up with rope.
Yours is too fat to lift.
Mine is falling to bits,
yours intact.

We won't invite the other for coffee
and we both know why;

we don't want to double the weight of guilt
and we can't come up with solutions.
We are out of solutions.

Crows line up on top of the caravan.
Dogs bark when they walk by the house.
When the time comes
and I go under I won't
tell about his body;
his body is his burden.
Mine's not even much of a body;
it's a mess.

I sleep in the loft now.
I feel it under me all the time.
I make a cup of tea and take two sips
and then I pour it down the drain;
I smoke a couple of cigarettes
and fall asleep
for a couple of hours.
I don't have anywhere to be.
Sirens sound in the distance

but I know they're not coming for me.
I put on my coat and run to the cash machine
but there's no money.
I go to the supermarket with loose change and have a panic attack.
I walk home;
nobody looks at me anymore.

I read books and when I spot something I don't like
I talk it through with myself.
I sit cross legged on the rough floorboards
with a pink cushion in my lap.
Sometimes I spray a bit of perfume.
I'm amazed that this body doesn't talk back.

When I get a phonecall I chew my lip
and stay quiet
so it is awkward for the other person;

I don't want anyone to think I'm happy.
At night I sometimes wake
to noises that seem to come from the body.
Mostly it's the shower weeping
or a branch against the window.

The sky is awash like glue.
I don't know what I'll do.
I think I will have to lie down
and take my tablets so quiet and good.
I don't think anyone wants this body back.
No-one has come looking for it.

# Group Therapy

We sat back in our chairs, shivering.
Our eyes turned to soft gold.
Ian said it happened in prison.
Deirdre said he broke into her room.
David said it was his psychiatrist, in the swinging seventies.
Deirdre said it's never about sex, but dominance.
We fell silent as we contemplated this.

Deirdre said she had not been able to stop fucking.
She's been fucking all her friends,
her family friends, anyone that talked to her.
She said it was the day that ended all the fucking.

My face was so tight, like a helium balloon.
I was hot inside, like the sap in a young tree, but
my skin grew cold, clammy and I didn't want anyone to touch me;
felt like such a cliché.

The receptionist didn't smile at us
and didn't like us smoking hungrily in the doorway.
We were all dying in that room, with tea and biscuits.
As we let go of those thoughts, the names for those memories,
it was as though something like shame
locked us down, locked our racing hearts back down.

I didn't have it as bad as some of the others.

That's what we did; by process of elimination
we discovered who had it worst
and we fancied that we might pray for them
if we were religious, and not just manic depressives.

# Play

I know the hunger will come and it will break you.
You have wet dreams because I won't play.
This is the fourth poem I have ever written
in which I will use the word sterile.
We don't need protection.
We just need faith,
some kind of angel.

In the room next door our children are playing with their food.
They are waiting for me to snap.
They don't know that the real politics in this house
are going on right now
in an empty, dark room with a cold, empty bed
where poltergeists are howling noiselessly
swinging from the lampshades,
mad for us.

The hunger will come and it will define you.
It was there before, when we met,
when even forests weren't too big for us.
I tell you I don't care if they eat, they won't starve.
You, on the other hand, are dying in a way nobody can see.
You're losing all your best years.
It's hard to bear witness to that, when in fact I cannot,
I cannot be without you.

There are no stars tonight, only rain.
I can't tune into the way you make me feel.
I have no clue when you will tire of my holding your head at night,
still as salt and mortar,
no clue when you will tire of me,
twist my arm
and break.

# Compassion

When you fall asleep you flinch and start for the first few minutes.
That's how I know you have gone. I dream that nobody wants
to come around here anymore. I dream that we are on our own.
You walk around the shops in the rain trying to stop yourself crying
for all the pain in the world, war, rape, hate. Now
everything upsets you; even my books, even me. I told you last night
that I regret everything except you and the children. All else
can go to Hell. You said you had regrets too, but you wouldn't tell.
You used to cry at the state of my arms, my war wounds, my tiger stripes.
They feel like leather, like voodoo.
You have become acclimatised to this, this pain, these scars
that hark back to a time before you. We can be pale. We can be damned.
We can be numb. We can let the heat in. We can let truth in. We can.
Everywhere I turn there are emotionally sterile people. We're not allowed
to walk around the shopping centre on the verge of tears.
Being inside your skin is too real. I have to grit my teeth to withstand it.
Your blood and your veins pulse all over me like clocks
ticking in my temples. You are riddled with sensitivity.
But we mustn't show it to them honey. All of my years are smashed up.
A twister whipped up my hummingbird heart. And I walked
away unscathed, forgot myself. I have said
too much. My darling, you wake so easily.

# Square Man

You're a square man. Everything about you is
square: your face, your chin, your body,
the squareness of your opinions,
the squareness of your emotional life.
With so many sides and corners you can bump
it away, the pains and the conflicts and the history:
bump bump bump.
We love you, square man.
We eat the round food you make for us,
chocolate puddings and cakes
too round to fit inside you whole:
we eat cream cream cream.
Your brother and sister were triangles.
You fitted together, three in a bed, you,
the little square-head in the middle.
When they died suddenly, you bumped it away:
bump bump bump.
You have never talked about it, never could.
When you go away
we get a square hug; we can put our arms around
your sides and you pat us and pat us with your
large square hands.

# Hanging On

Occasionally we sit on the veranda and drink stewed tea
from an old pot. It hasn't stopped snowing for days.
I have bare legs and two black coats, a pair of unlaced boots.
You watch me; I feel like I'm being filmed.

The wind whips up and it's like the place will turn over,
roll around in the brush and collapse trees in its wake.
We get inside and we don't know what to do
except touch one another.

You know my daughter hasn't lived with me for a year
and that I've never come down.
You know the routine of pills, appointments.
I have accepted that you will not stay forever.

I have all these plans, to get Betsy back,
to straighten out, to get well, to love.
You are going to America for a few months;
it's going to spell heartbreak, like in a 1950s film,

only I'll end up in the kitchen with a knife at my wrists
when I'm supposed to be chopping vegetables.
It hurts to be as close as this. It's what I always wanted
but I never expected the terror of it, love —

love, love, you are no drug, you are deadlier.

I don't sleep next to you, I wander about, inert. Outside,
where you'd expect to find a dead body,
wild horses and deer roam like royalty.

You sleep fitfully. In the morning I rattle, I'm sick
and my thoughts race; my mind is stuck with electrodes.
I don't want you to wake up, so I can be in love forever,
tousling your hair and hanging on, no plan or daydream, just nothing.

# Major Organs

When they take my brain out of its casing
it will be fluorescent
and the mortuary assistant will stand back
because it will dazzle so brightly.
My brain will be heavier than a watermelon
and shot with gold.

I want them to remove everything.
I want to be an empty shell.
They won't be able to give my lungs away
and my heart won't be strong enough
to get someone through the next decade
but I want to be packed with gauze
and something to take the smell away.

When I die I want to be clean.
I want someone to say
I am the cleanest woman they've ever examined.
I want them to oil my brain before they put it back in.
Loosen my tongue
and stitch me with catgut and parcel string.

Because I won't be coming back,
butterflies will avoid my grave,
my agitated foot will cease to tap
and every time someone plays my favourite song

my heart will beat twice as fast
in some poor person to whom they didn't tell
my heartache, its poor diet of pain.

My kidneys
won't miss me. My liver is in top notch condition,
crushed velvet all the way through.
I don't want them to take my eyes;
they'll roll in the back of someone's head.
My arms and legs will fold clumsily inside the box
like a puppet afraid of its master.

# Fettered Heart

They don't know what it does to my brain.
I don't feel it, wet and thin, lubricating,
sliding in and out of holes that have been there
since I opened my mouth.

The Lord moves in mysterious ways.
He gives me an injection every week
in a chaotic clinic full of the clinically insane
who are in shock all of the time.

Melvyn stares at his appointment card
for ten minutes. He tells someone his dad is dead.
He is eager to get his injection
so he can go shopping, and maybe today he won't cry.

All the women are fat.
The nurses don't have to be so careful with the needle.
Plenty of room in our buffalo behinds.
The drugs are stored up in red, raw muscle.

I have a stiff mouth, I am curt.
I can't go back to listening to Death's answerphone.
I can't go back to arching my back like I'm falling
out of an aeroplane; the contortions, the shape-shifting;

the hospitals, the pills, the vomit, the hallucinations,

and the locked doors, the stale beds, the absence
of myself. And the rain today is freezing just as soon as it settles.
I have been skidding around like a lunatic in my plastic shoes.

I am attuned. I bleed out.
I pick up on rhythms, abnormalities.
I pick up on the language of gratitude and servility.
And I am not a pretty girl.

We are not pretty people. We are living like the slack-jawed fish
that swim around coral reefs, being maintained.
I wait patiently, every day, for something to prove this ordinary
life is part of something extraordinary.

Nothing happens. I take the shot, I whip up
my knickers, they ask me if I'm well and I say well, *yes*.
I am not connected. There are no ordinary words for these things.
I am not connected to the world as in outside my head

or the world as it is inside my five year old son's brain.
I could easily believe that nothing bad will ever happen.
Maybe the strength of our delusion is the true test of happiness.
My son announces when he grows up he's going to get rich

while Melvyn at the clinic is content with being presentable.
He wears a shirt and tie on an average day.
(No employment, no place to be.
Nowhere. I think I admire him.)

There are old tears swimming in my head like larvae.
I would pluck each one with tweezers.
I have tried to extract them before,
sad songs, bad poems, the five o'clock news

streaming like radiation. I don't wish for damnation
but I haven't cried in three years and my eyes are dry
and the drugs have settled in the ducts.
I piss antipsychotics. I piss tears and tea,

endless tea and endless darkness winding around my veins.
When I walk to his school I imagine falling
on the ice and breaking all my bones, and having to
get onto my broken knees with my broken hands

and my wrists snapping and my head caving in.
I imagine this broken person walking into school
scaring the shit out of the children.
Bits falling off. An ear, a crumpled finger.

But I don't break. I stay fat and whole like an almond
left out of the pan. Everything's contagious. You should know
that if I came to your house with a loose tongue
and five species of Amazonian birds to peck at your head

you *will* catch something. You will find it in something I said.
I have worked hard at living. You don't have to
work so hard at death. I have enough sleeping pills in my house
to kill myself. But it's not the dark that shames me;

I am see-through, flat shoes and a coat
that puts on two dress sizes. You don't smile back
because my lungs are on the outside, heaving.
Nobody wants to see that.

Everyone is too polite to say,
and I bleed into my pockets and it dribbles
onto the pavement and from my nose
and I imagine myself in white

with white blood and white kidneys.
Melvyn doesn't mind. He sees his own insides all the time and he
smiles fondly at mine. The glitter in his blood is the residue
from the drugs, collecting, sparkling.

People now don't know what they want; they are not aware of
their own mortality; they can get in a car dreaming
of California, hot women and hot sex.
They can cross the road striding like The Beatles did.

I know what I want. My brain free again, not held
hostage; not tortured, force fed. If I am to be mad
then so be it. Those hospitals cannot keep me anymore,
I have outgrown them, outwitted them, they're not so clever,

those doctors cannot rein me in. My son is drawing
birds with crayons. He's colour blind.
My world is not fluorescent today. Here, there is no colour,

no competition with the sun.

See how I shift through time and space, it's magnificent.
I can be anywhere. This chair, this table;
a whole week. A week like the lining up of pills
on the bedside table. The bulb burning out;

lying on my back in the dark thinking about stars
and death, and death and stars.
I am not mediocre. But nobody knows what it does to the brain.
Nobody knows what they're doing.

Melvyn skips mentally along down the road to his favourite shop
where the check-out girl smiles and his shirt has no creases.
I pine after my husband to come and save me before I rip
my hands open in the kitchen scourer,

washing and washing the bloody place as though
madness has infected it. The air outside is crisp.
They keep telling me it'll snow but it doesn't.
They keep telling me it's all to make me better;

the taxpayer pays for my drugs. I am emotionally inarticulate.
No fights to fight, just getting rest, emotional regulation,
free from stress, no phone-calls, no excitement. This is dangerous,
this is dangerous. From nowhere —

I fall off the doorstep   I fall off the bed   I fall
from the passenger seat    I fall on the shop floor    I fall

down the staircase     I fall in the street
I fall down in the clinic     I fall from the sky

I land on my head     on my head     on my head.

# Suicide

There's a child, a pretty girl. We all see her. The nurses don't.
Sarah calls her Mary. She won't talk to us.
She is always trying to loosen the reinforced windows for us.
She scratches at the dulled panes,
has a terrible hacking cough; we listen to it all night long.

Sarah says Mary's only five and her mother doesn't want her.
I want her. I don't drink and I don't eat. And Sarah's mad,
madder than television, than torchlight at the back of your eyes;
we spend all day going out of our minds like scratched records
                                   skipping.
Sometimes I see whole days in and out of this chair.
Mary, she climbs up onto the roof and we hear her laughter.

I want to follow her.
Nobody will miss Mary; I clutch at my knee and I howl after her,
her little legs and grazed knees no-one will ever kiss.
Outside it's gale force, she'll never make it.
The wind picks up and smashes and smashes against the
                                   dormitories;
my hands shatter in my lap. Sarah says it's ok,
someone will come soon and sweep them up.

# Elizabeth's Bed

They said we could have the bed for nothing.
It was a firm, floral bed.
The fabric slightly bobbled where
her dainty hip had lain.
I imagined her dying in a foetal position
though mostly we think of old folks
dying on their back,
or in a chair with their heads cocked to the side.
I worried that it would give her
bad dreams, even though
she was only three and didn't know;
I worried that somehow death
would unpeel itself from the mattress
and merge with her shadow, the hawk-black of her irises,
dance along with her where she skipped down the road.

# Levi

You can see jellyfish pink-blue veins in Angie's arms and chest.
Her heart flutters like she's swum too far out at sea. She
is afraid she'll die with the weight on her heart;
we are all afraid of it.
Levi drank a bottle of vodka and
inhaled butane gas and
pulled tight the noose and
jumped over the side of the bridge.
Angie's mother took her there after the funeral.
There were flowers laid, and all she could think of
was the crack of his young neck breaking,
the blood inside of him coagulating.
And suddenly mortality reveals itself to us, us asylum girls —
we have stepped back from the edge.
Angie is wearing black this month,
she couldn't be any slimmer,
though she's off the drip and her appetite's better-
other lads are interested in her,
the hug of her human bones.
She tells me about them, and about how many sit-ups
she can do on home leave when her parents aren't watching.
I am afraid to touch her in case she falls to dust.
I am afraid to touch her in case she wants me to.
Levi is not coming back even though she's made out with his ghost.
Levi has left the building.
Levi couldn't give a stuff about coming back to haunt us.

He is making his way down to the Lethe
where her name will form a bubble and fly out of his mouth
in a hiccup. His body is black like the skin of a polar bear.
He has died many times, he has drowned.
We all try to remember how to pray for his soul,
our hands to our lips, not sure how death came down in the night
and touched us, and wanted for us.

# On Mount Mihara

*Once a popular place for suicides*


When I was six I let go my mother's hand
whenever I could. I wriggled it loose. She gave in
after a time and let me walk on my own.

I liked to let go. I liked to dive into the pool both hands
above my head and cup the water as I swam —
plunging headlong, I could push away from myself endlessly.

I didn't hold my boyfriend's hand;
it was so big and it stifled mine. I got upset
if too many people embarked on the train and I had to

stand between them. They couldn't hold me back
when the time came. There was no-one
at the summit and I wanted to fly.

I imagined my body as a red hot coal,
rolling down a hill in the sun, smoke billowing.
No-one could touch me,

hold my hand, or keep me from being free.
Liquid and ash, all beautiful, bright
and spilling from me.

# Town Show '82

The photograph is all the colours of a headache;
muted, almost sepia, a khaki sleeveless jacket, a belt, a camera,
you smoking over my mother's shoulder.
Hot blood collects behind my eyes.
Until my eleventh year you were dead. Not there
in the misplaced picture in your plimsoll shoes and fat silver watch
you probably couldn't afford.
I want to be inside this frame, between the two white billygoats,
burn the show tent down, stand in the ashes and say
daddy, it matters not where you have been,
if you come with me now I will write you poems,
push you around in a wheelchair in your old age.
I will sit with you around hospital beds,
contract MRSA and light your cigarettes.
I scan every last centimetre now as though it holds a clue.
Joe, your name is Joe.

# I'll Find You

You could be writing a journal, all the days of our absence
accounted for. You could be swimming in a lake.
You could be making your confession, the smell of old wood.
You could be reciting poems, the apple not falling far from the tree.
You could be in a hospital bed pumped full of morphine.
You could be ballroom dancing with a skinny woman in red,
your heart waltzing. You could be lying
in some back street, long hair knotted with ash and puke.
You could be stealing from under their noses. You could be
waiting for a bus that's an hour late and you're wet through.
You could be in bed with man flu. You could be laughing
with your other, younger children. You could be swimming
with sharks, somewhere in the world where you won't find us
though you never stopped looking. You could be holding a knife
in one hand, a glass of beer in the other. You could be
walking a tightrope. You could be making dinner for four,
crying as you dice an onion. You could be arguing
with your mistress about calling your phone during dinner.
You could be on the psych ward — hallucinating,
refusing the pills. You could be reclining on a beach in Italy.
You could be thinking about me, tell me you've been thinking
about me. You could be half cut, you could be broke. You
could be charged with assault, you could be imprisoned,
staring at that crumpled photo of us from the eighties.
You could be talking on your phone about starting from scratch,
tapping figures into a computer in an office on the sixth floor.

You could be dead. You could be dead in a hospital bed,
dead indoors, dead through misadventure, or pneumonia,
or drinking your own weight, or falling in front of a train.
Dead. You could be being resuscitated, could be fighting
for your life. You could be thinking about pouring yourself
a cup of tea to go with your cigarette, listening to the radio;
or sleeping. You could just be sleeping.

# Bringing You Home

I looked at the flat where you died on a digital photograph.
A four-storey whitewashed house with starlings
nesting in the gutters, bay windows and plenty of light.

I imagined you were painting a masterpiece there,
by the seafront, living off Nescafe and fish and chips.
Mum reckoned you'd gone there to convalesce;

Colwyn Bay was like that in the nineties.
I plan to travel to this place that I don't know,
get to know the geography, not just this architecture of dreams;

a whitewashed house has receded into my unconscious.
Here the landscape is different but I feel
you could have benefited from the warmth of strangers

and not just the tobacconists and dealers.
I am bringing you home to me,
carrying you all these miles with my viscera,

flying you in through an open window and putting you
to bed. If you stay dead I will read you poems.
I will walk for miles with prayers in my heart like coronary balloons

filling with hot blood. It's heavy, this bereavement
twelve years delayed. I walk with a dual longing

for life and for death. I pace up the council estate on the outskirts

to the suburbs where we could never afford to live,
blackbirds squabbling in the brambles.
I walk to the war memorial where we used to go drinking as kids

because it was lit up at night; the tree we carved our names on
has been felled. Some things here die without a trace.
I've come so far to find you. Your daughters

didn't attend your funeral. They didn't lay flowers or grieve.
Tonight I walk to my first boyfriend's red-brick house where
we would smoke roll-ups out of the window on school days,

it has been up for sale five times in two years.
His dad bled to death there. His stepdad kept a gun. I believe
that the sublimated energy of a place can carry on

over miles and miles and into your arms whether you heed it or not.
The photograph is all I've got but you've become so indefinable
in my mind that when I sleep I am peeling back bed-sheets,

unlocking cold eyelids and knees; I am stood
at the window staring out at the sea I cannot connect with
in my world of woods where kids make fires and get wasted

and still waters which are the shadow of death
and open plains which are the shadow of death
and dilapidated buildings which are the shadow of death.

# Belly

When I was fifteen I took my two little cousins into town
and had them wait outside the tattoo parlour
while a woman with blue hair pierced my belly button
with a big red ruby that pooled inside like a roving eye.
They were crying when I emerged.
I was hardly able to breathe for fear of the pain.
On the way home on the bus, Amy sang 'Karma Chameleon'
and Simone looked out of the window at time passing
as though watching something being silently obliterated.
I remember my belly looked so white and soft lying down
with the jewellery collecting like a well of fresh blood.
I thought it quite beautiful though it often snagged
on my jeans. My girlfriend had once rooted the ruby out with her
tongue; the next morning had stung. When we found
a baby kicking in there I had to take the jewellery
out as my teenage belly stretched. Having that metal
inside my body had been as good as a wound. My girlfriend and I
had wounds to nurse, they comforted, they reassured;
while they healed there was a warm place inside
devoted to new cells and plasma.
After the birth, my belly was a waste of space,
a forlorn temple with no jewel or way in.
I couldn't accept the tender map of pain
left imprinted on my belly when my baby was born.
I would trace the stubborn, soft pulse
of a network of trails in my deep skin with my fingers,

willing and willing them to recede.
Nobody touched my belly then, not for a decade.
My belly was women's business. My belly was the place
a baby once lived. If I was carrion my belly would be
the first flesh to peck and rip — my most vulnerable part —
silvery white in sunlight, nobody's prize. The little nick
of a piercing scar reminds me that I'm not fifteen anymore.
My daughter has only once asked me about my
numerous scars, about the little black rose tattoo on my back
that scabbed and skewed. Her belly is small and smooth like a chalice.
White, like mine, but pure, hollow, unpunctured.
One day she will go to the tattoo parlour
just to have something done to her. Just to see if it hurts.
Just to feel something healing over.

# Home Leave

Your car is pillar-box red.
Nobody will die in it.
I sit by your side and say nothing, my hands
bunched in fists in my lap.
When the lights turn
I feel you breathing.
The motorway gapes.
We are on our way to the hospital
where they greet me like a donor,
like I'm giving away both my eyes.
You are happy
when I come home with something bandaged
it looks like someone has done something.
Some weekends I come home to you.
I fill in the form
that says I don't feel guilty, hopeless or paranoid.
We watch TV until I fall asleep
and we go to bed
like children after hot milk.
You think you have done something wrong.
I don't tell you otherwise.
In the morning
you pop my pills into a decanter,
a little pink plastic box
with all the days of the week.
You lock the pills in the safe.

In the heart of a safe those pills
can't call out to me.
I can't be tempted and
you will not be to blame.
I write poems in the hospital.
There are fourteen of us staring at walls
and scratched reinforced windows
that don't let in the sun.
We put too many sugars in our tea
and don't listen to anything.
Not anything that you can hear.
I pray to God.
I pray for mercy or a knife.
You come with clothes and I
brush my hair for you —
for a moment you look so happy.
I sit on your knee laughing
until my chest hurts.

# Last Night You Took Your First Sleeping Pill

I love the way you smooth yourself down
with cologne each morning,
alkaline for your rosy skin, lambs-wool catching
on your dry hands.

Last night I dreamt about a chicken carcass
teeming with fat maggots.
I woke and realised you were gone
and my brain was teeming. I had a pain
in my stomach like poison.

You're always so clean.
Your leavened heart is clean;
your blood is purer than mine
muddy with cholesterol and lithium.

If only we had been eaten by wild animals
in the forests of Inverness.
If only we didn't have to feel this sadness
in our sleep. How you lie awake,
a drumbeat in your head

masking my heartbeat. We came to this place
where all the colours are the same every day
except when it rains. We wanted this
security, this strange blue mood

we live beneath.

When it rains we remember
how we used to fuck in the shower
and how we don't do that anymore
how we are immersed

in the maintenance of ourselves.
Tonight the town is flooding and I want to
look into you,
like you're a storm coming
and there's no turning back,
like I've no clue,

but you gather me up,
the hems of my skirt,
the kinks in my hair, and I fold into the bed,
into your arms, like an unanswered letter.

# My Lovelies

I had a vivid imagination.
We lived behind a factory
that blocked out the sun.
My mother would stitch old ladies' slippers in silence,
my new teeth cutting through
with the quick taste of blood that I savoured.
I suspected I was not the only girl
of my kind.

My sister warned me about vampires
when I was six, and I lost my pig heart
in an old wooden box filled with dismembered teddies.
The foam innards irritated the flesh.

I would climb into my sister's moody bed,
where the dark sneaked under the covers like smoke
as I lifted them so quietly —
her cold legs wouldn't fasten with mine
and when I woke her
she'd rage and shout and push me out
to go and sleep with the rotten vampires.

But the vampires grew to love me.
They lay with me like fathers, sons.
Sometimes I would wrap my legs around them,
my pussy pushed up against their thighs,

and I would pray for them.
I had a vivid imagination, my mother said.
But I suspected I was not the only one.

When I stayed in his house I took
my beloved vampires with me to suck
on his rubber neck — to suck, to suck.
But he was impenetrable.
And I had a vivid imagination.

# Dimensions

I become more afraid of your body every year. Its tenderness
and its strength squeeze me down to a little cube of love,
all sides shimmering and melting at once;

Every year I become more afraid of your body,
of your almond skin that breaks a sweat like the first droplets
from a dam. Behind your skin there's an ocean.

Your body, every year, is becoming more afraid.
My colours are fading because you have licked them,
and one day you will not rouse me when I wake in colour.

All of me and all of you drinks of the fear in my heart.
Erasure is never complete. I try to imagine you without a body.
In the heat of the night we sing like tin.

# Peter Pan

I was naked from my shower
and you climbed from the bed where you were taking a nap
and came up behind me, your legs
straddling my legs,
and you stilled me and kissed my neck and shoulders
like they were worth an awful lot of money.
My hair got in my eyes
and my lips rooted for your skin.
Later, we had to take Zopiclone to sleep,
at one in the morning;
you had been sat up in bed eating chocolate and
reading Capote, quietly chuckling.
The city outside of us
breathed;
we could see its breath on the windows.
When I am with you
I'm beside myself because I can't have you
completely, and although
you give yourself to me completely
I can't have you and I'm beside myself.

## That Afternoon We Listened to Sparklehorse and Thought About Dying

On the fourth floor we looked out at factories, Autumn's eccentricity
elevating the determination of grey. We couldn't
feel anything. We smoked until we were numb.
I fell asleep. The baby slept an hour and a half in the pram.
My head rested on your shoulder. You took my weight, held me.
I'd been to the weigh-and-save for a cup of sugar
and what little meal I could afford. You made me
a cup of tea strong enough to wake me;
played with the baby while I came round sipping at the steam.
There was beauty in every movement you made; your earphones
perpetually stuck in your ears to kill
or soothe the voices. How I loved you. How I
didn't care if you stole from the shop I worked in.
You had sex for your fix, though you denied it. Though you put
your arms around me. You existed in a parallel universe
I sometimes crossed over into. Your silences rolled around my tongue.
They were a language of their own — we'd roll and smoke cigarettes
in unison. Your neighbour had died from self-inflicted
stab wounds. You recounted the story to me
as though you had been in the room, smelt the blood.
His girlfriend had died at the wheel of a car.
She was going into labour, on her way home, Christmas Eve.
You know and I know how messy life can get
when you mess with it, when you push your luck.
I stepped out that day with clear eyes, a creased dress

and a hankering for sex and cigarettes and hot food.
As it was, I caught the bus and had the not-so-fleeting thought
that I might never see you again.